W9-CSJ-513

WITH SAWN

Sherman, Jill,
All about online gaming
/
[2017] WITHDRAWN
33305238900751
mh   10/25/17

ALL ABOUT ONLINE GAMING

by Jill Sherman

FOCUS
READERS

North Star
EDITIONS

WWW.NORTHSTAREDITIONS.COM

Copyright © 2017 by North Star Editions, Lake Elmo, MN 55042. All rights reserved. No part of this book may be reproduced or utilized in any form or by any means without written permission from the publisher.

Produced for North Star Editions by Red Line Editorial.

Photographs ©: Kiko Jimenez/Shutterstock Images, cover, 1; charnsitr/Shutterstock Images, 4–5; Ted S. Warren/AP Images, 7; omihay/Shutterstock Images, 8–9; Louis-Paul St-Onge/iStockphoto, 10; Uber Images/Shutterstock Images, 12; dny3d/Shutterstock Images, 15; Donald Traill/Invision for EA Sports/AP Images, 16–17; Dean Drobot/Shutterstock Images, 18; g-stockstudio/iStockphoto, 20–21; mirafoto imagebroker/Newscom, 23; Margot Petrowski/Shutterstock Images, 25; betto rodrigues/Shutterstock Images, 26–27; Matthew Corley/Shutterstock Images, 29

Content Consultant: Dr. Kurt Squire, Professor of Curriculum and Instruction, University of Wisconsin–Madison

ISBN
978-1-63517-013-9 (hardcover)
978-1-63517-069-6 (paperback)
978-1-63517-174-7 (ebook pdf)
978-1-63517-124-2 (hosted ebook)

Library of Congress Control Number: 2016949756

Printed in the United States of America
Mankato, MN
November, 2016

ABOUT THE AUTHOR

Jill Sherman lives and writes in Brooklyn, New York. She has written dozens of books for young people. She enjoys researching new topics and is thrilled by all the new technologies that bring gamers together online. Jill is training to run a 10K and enjoys taking photos of her dog.

TABLE OF CONTENTS

CHAPTER 1

A Second Life 5

CHAPTER 2

Kinds of Games 9

HOW IT WORKS

Gamers Connect 14

CHAPTER 3

Building a Better World 17

CHAPTER 4

The Dark Side 21

CHAPTER 5

The Future of Gaming 27

Focus on Online Gaming • 30
Glossary • 31
To Learn More • 32
Index • 32

A SECOND LIFE

Trekking across a dense forest, you guide your orc to the meeting place. You are preparing for battle. Your fellow guild members have already arrived. Trolls, undead, elves, and goblins have all gathered. You know that many of these people live in different parts of the United States.

Modern consoles such as the PlayStation 4 enable gamers to play online.

Some are even from other countries. But here in the game, you are all together. Lifting your sword, you join your team and launch into battle.

For decades, the only way to compete with other gamers was to have friends visit. But today, most video games have at least some online pieces. Personal computers (PCs), modern game **consoles**, and mobile devices all connect to the Internet.

Playing online creates a community. Often, players can chat with each other while playing. When games go online, it's good for **developers** as well. They can fix bugs, or problems, in the game. They can

Crowds gather to watch a video game tournament.

also add expansions, which extend the game with new maps, missions, and other features. The Internet makes great things possible for players and developers alike.

CHAPTER 2

KINDS OF GAMES

Whether you play on a console, PC, smartphone, or tablet, you can take part in online gaming. All the major console systems encourage players to use their online services. Xbox Live, Nintendo Network, and PlayStation Network let gamers play and chat with others.

Minecraft is a popular game that lets players build worlds out of cubes.

Headsets allow gamers to talk to other people while playing.

Another common way to play online is through browser-based games. No expensive **software** is needed. The game plays in whatever browser the player uses to view websites. Many times, these are simple games such as *Slither.io*. But more complicated games, such as *Forge of Empires*, are also possible.

Apps are similar to browser-based games. Users can download games to their mobile devices. *Candy Crush Saga*, *Pokémon Go*, and *Angry Birds* are some of the most popular app-based games. Players can log their scores and compete against their friends.

PLAYING SOLDIER

First-person shooters are a common type of online game. Typically, players take the role of a soldier, often in a science fiction universe. Players and their teammates use strategy to battle enemy soldiers. In contrast, real-time strategy (RTS) games let players command entire armies against one another. These games are usually not meant for children.

Programming languages such as Scratch enable kids to create their own games.

Massively multiplayer online games (MMOs) are one of the most popular kinds of online games. In these games, thousands of players are online at once. One of the most popular MMOs is *World of Warcraft*. At its peak, *World of Warcraft* had 12 million subscribers. This game has a rating of Teen.

Through the Internet, each player logs in to the game's **servers**. This is where the game is hosted. MMOs have a social aspect to them. All players are accessing the same world. That means players can chat and team up with one another.

GAMERS CONNECT

Gamers can connect with one another in a variety of ways. They may use their computers, consoles, or mobile devices to play online games. Whatever device they use, it must be able to connect to the Internet.

Once the gamer is online, he or she can then connect to the server that hosts the game. Thousands of gamers connect to the same server at the same time. This enables people from all around the globe to play within the same digital world at once.

Whenever a gamer connects to the Internet, his or her device communicates with a server.

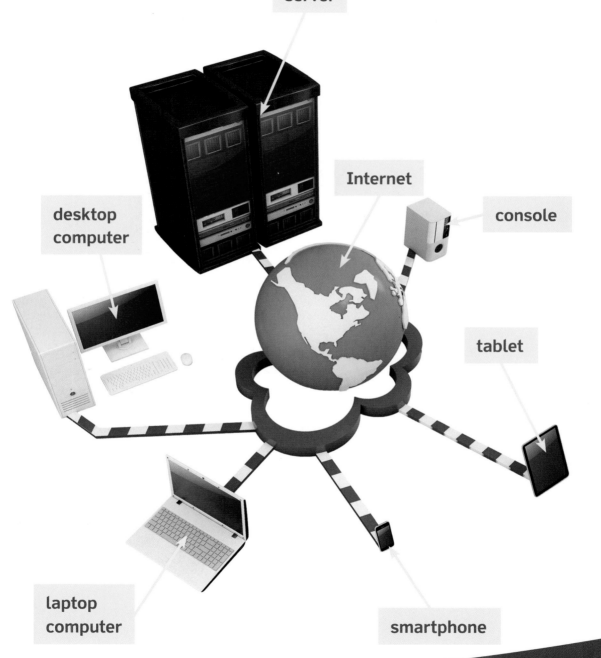

server

Internet

console

desktop
computer

tablet

laptop
computer

smartphone

CHAPTER 3

BUILDING A BETTER WORLD

Putting games online makes them available to people around the world. This is good for both players and developers. Players have access to a huge variety of games. Developers can reach more people who want to play their games. They don't have to manufacture the games and get stores to sell them.

Sports games are extremely popular with online gamers.

Many games are available as demos, enabling users to try a game before buying it.

People who buy the online versions of games sometimes get special perks. Companies often release exclusive content to online users. Online gamers may get special characters or missions that other gamers miss out on.

Gaming teaches valuable skills, too. Teamwork and strategy are important to winning many online games. Some studies have even linked game play to improved grades. Succeeding in a role-playing game requires reading, teamwork, and thinking scientifically.

GAMIFICATION

Scientists have **gamified** some of their research projects. For example, researchers wanted to figure out the different shapes that **proteins** could fold into. Knowing these shapes helps scientists understand diseases and figure out cures. Researchers created a game called *Foldit*, in which players score points by creating models of protein shapes. Already, *Foldit* has helped scientists better understand the AIDS virus.

CHAPTER 4

THE DARK SIDE

Bugs, **glitches**, and slow connections can cause problems with online games. Developers are continually working to **patch** these problems. But the fixes require gamers to install constant updates. In some cases, a company may have to take the entire game down while making repairs.

Bugs and glitches can cause major frustrations for gamers.

Also, by buying games online, players no longer have the same ownership as when they purchase copies in stores. The games get downloaded to their consoles or computers. Gamers cannot sell games they are finished with. They cannot swap games with their friends. Also, a company may take down an online game. That means the game is gone, even if people spent money on it.

Online gaming also comes at a cost. Some games require a subscription. Each month, players have to pay if they want to continue to play the game. Free-to-play games have their costs as well. These games encourage players to purchase

Gamers play at a video game convention.

in-game resources. Without realizing it, many players can rack up a large bill.

Online gaming can also have negative effects on players' lives. Some gamers spend many hours a day in online worlds that are different from their real lives.

They make friends and feel accepted. But in the real world, gamers may still spend a lot of time alone. As a result, some gamers may let other parts of their lives suffer because they find their digital lives so satisfying.

GOLD FARMING

In some games, collecting in-game currency is free and is a part of regular game play. However, collecting currency can be time-consuming for most players. So, players sometimes exchange in-game resources for real cash. Entire businesses have been developed around "gold farming." Rather than playing the game, users spend the bulk of their time gathering resources to sell. Many games have banned selling in-game currency.

Keeping personal information private helps gamers stay safe online.

Privacy and violence and are two other concerns. Gamers should be careful not to give out personal information such as name, age, and location. They should also get an adult's permission before playing violent games. Some studies have suggested that playing violent video games increases aggression.

CHAPTER 5

THE FUTURE OF GAMING

Game developers are always looking for ways to create games that are new and exciting. One trend that has been making its way into people's homes is virtual reality (VR) technology. Players can strap on a headset and feel as if they have entered a new world.

Virtual reality headsets hold the promise of more immersive gaming experiences.

When the player turns her head, she sees more of the digital world around her. She can even see her digital arms swinging a sword or shooting an arrow. As VR technology improves, it will take players even deeper into digital worlds.

Another big change in gaming is the use of secondary screens. Players can use a handheld screen in addition to the main screen. The Wii U GamePad and Xbox SmartGlass are some examples. The second screen lets players keep playing while they check their inventory or the game map.

As Internet connections become even faster, more games will become possible

Augmented reality (AR) games such as *Pokémon Go* are played in the real world on mobile devices.

online. Games will become easier to access. Through online games, more people will be able to connect to the worlds and stories they love.

FOCUS ON
ONLINE GAMING

Write your answers on a separate piece of paper.

1. Write a sentence that describes the key ideas from Chapter 3.

2. Do you think it's a problem that some gamers spend a lot of time alone? Why or why not?

3. What is one of the most popular MMOs?

    A. *Pokémon Go*
    B. *World of Warcraft*
    C. *Angry Birds*

4. Which of these is a benefit of browser-based games?

    A. Players do not have to buy expensive software.
    B. Players can sell their games when they are finished.
    C. Players are required to pay for a subscription.

Answer key on page 32.

GLOSSARY

consoles
Computer systems made specifically for video games.

developers
People who make and design video games.

gamified
Turned nongame tasks into a game.

glitches
Unexpected problems in a computer program.

patch
To fix an error in computer code that causes a bug.

proteins
Molecules that are important in telling a living cell what to do.

servers
Computers that make data or programs available to other computers.

software
Programs that run on a computer.

TO LEARN MORE

BOOKS

Adamson, Heather. *Inventing the Video Game*. Mankato, MN: The Child's World, 2016.

Funk, Joe. *Hot Jobs in Video Games: Cool Careers in Interactive Entertainment*. New York: Scholastic, 2010.

Gimpel, Diane Marczely. *Violence in Video Games*. Minneapolis: Abdo Publishing, 2013.

NOTE TO EDUCATORS

Visit **www.focusreaders.com** to find lesson plans, activities, links, and other resources related to this title.

INDEX

Angry Birds, 11

browser-based games, 10–11
bugs, 6

Candy Crush Saga, 11
consoles, 6, 9, 14, 22

developers, 6–7, 17, 21, 27

expansions, 7

Foldit, 19
Forge of Empires, 10

gamification, 19
gold farming, 24

massively multiplayer online games, 13

Nintendo Network, 9

ownership, 22

patches, 21
PCs, 6, 9
PlayStation Network, 9
Pokémon Go, 11
privacy, 25

secondary screens, 28
servers, 13, 14
Slither.io, 10

violence, 25
virtual reality, 27–28

Wii U GamePad, 28
World of Warcraft, 13

Xbox Live, 9
Xbox SmartGlass, 28

Answer Key: 1. Answers will vary; **2.** Answers will vary; **3.** B; **4.** A